SMARTPHONE ADDICTION IT'S ENOUGH:

Unplugged yourself and Master the Art of Digital Detox

John Deon

DISCLAIMER

The information contained in this book is for general informational purposes only. While every effort has been made to ensure the accuracy and completeness of the content, the author and publisher make no representations or warranties of any kind, express or implied, about the completeness, accuracy, reliability, suitability, or availability with respect to the information, products, services, or related graphics contained in this book for any purpose.

Any reliance you place on such information is therefore strictly at your own risk. In no event will the author or publisher be liable for any loss or damage including without limitation, indirect or consequential loss or damage, or any loss or damage whatsoever arising from loss of data or profits arising out of, or in connection with, the use of this book. The inclusion of certain information, opinions, or recommendations within this book does not imply endorsement by the author or publisher.

This book may contain references to third-party websites, resources, or products. These references are provided for informational purposes only and do not imply endorsement or approval by the author or publisher. The author and publisher have no control over the nature, content, and availability of those sites or resources and are not responsible for any content, advertising, products, or other materials on or available from such sites or resources.

Every effort has been made to respect copyright laws and to properly attribute sources for any material used within this book. If any errors or omissions are found, please contact the author or publisher.

Table of Contents

Introduction

Josh was consistently the life of the party. With his contagious laughter and endless enthusiasm, he could brighten any room. He was the type of man who thrived on social engagements, eager to reconnect with friends and create new experiences. But as he approached his late twenties, Josh observed a subtle change in his behavior—one that would eventually take him down the path of addiction.

It all began simply enough. Josh, like many young adults, relied on his smartphone for daily duties including reading emails, communicating with friends, and navigating the city. But as the years passed, Josh found himself spending ever more time on his phone, idly browsing through social media feeds or becoming caught in endless rounds of mobile games.

Josh didn't take it very seriously at first. After all, everyone seemed to be addicted to their phones these days, so what damage could a little additional screen time cause? But as Josh's smartphone use increased, he noticed small changes in his attitude and conduct. When he was away from his phone, he became increasingly angry and impatient, and he would frequently experience anxiety when he missed a notice or text message.

Despite his rising anxieties, Josh was unable to break free from his smartphone. It had become a constant companion, providing both comfort and distraction in a world that appeared increasingly chaotic and unpredictable. He would spend hours each day idly looking through social media feeds, comparing his life to the meticulously manicured photos of others and experiencing feelings of inadequacy and FOMO.

Josh's relationships deteriorated as his smartphone addiction grew worse. He found himself ignoring his friends and family in favor of spending time on his phone, frequently canceling arrangements at the last minute or losing focus during talks. He understood deep down that his smartphone use was bad, but he couldn't seem to find the strength to change.

Josh only recognized he needed help when he hit rock bottom. One evening, while out with friends at a neighborhood pub, Josh found himself scrolling through his phone rather than conversing. As he looked up from his screen, he saw a sea of dejected faces looking back at him. It was a wake-up call—a sharp reminder of how his addiction had harmed his relationships and his own health.

Determined to make a difference, Josh set out on a path of self-discovery and healing. He sought help from friends and family, who provided encouragement and accountability. He also made a concerted effort to limit his screen time, establishing guidelines for when and when he may use his phone.

However, breaking free from smartphone addiction was not simple. Josh was tempted and self-conscious at times, and he considered quitting up and reverting to his old habits. But with each passing day, he grew stronger and more resilient, learning to put his mental and emotional health ahead of the transient distractions of his smartphone.

Josh gradually regained control of his life. He rediscovers the delight of face-to-face relationships, the simple pleasure of being present in the moment, free of the continual buzz of messages and alarms. He sought activities and interests that provided him with contentment and joy, seeking refuge in the beauty of the world outside of his smartphone screen.

And as he reflected on his path, Josh recognized that breaking free from smartphone addiction was more than just unplugging from his phone; it was also about reconnecting with himself and the world around him. It was a voyage of self-discovery and progress, demonstrating the power of perseverance and tenacity in the face of adversity.

Josh is happy and healthier than he's ever been. He still uses his smartphone, but it now functions as a tool rather than a crutch, allowing him to remain in touch with loved ones and access information that enhances his life. And as he looks ahead, Josh is filled with hope and appreciation, knowing that he has conquered one of his life's most difficult trials and come out stronger on the other side.

Chapter 1:
Understanding Smartphone Addiction

In today's fast-paced digital world, cellphones have transformed how we communicate, work, and engage with our surroundings. With their elegant appearance, strong capabilities, and continual connectivity, pocket-sized devices have become an essential aspect of modern life. However, in addition to their numerous benefits, cellphones pose a major danger of addiction.

What is Smartphone Addiction?

Smartphone addiction, also known as problematic smartphone usage or smartphone reliance, is a behavioral addiction defined by obsessive and excessive smartphone use, frequently at the expense of other aspects of life. Smartphone addiction, like other types of addiction, such as alcohol abuse or gambling, is characterized by a lack of control over one's conduct and a fixation on the gadget.

Smartphone addiction is fueled by the rapid reward and continual stimulation that cellphones offer. Smartphones provide a seemingly infinite array of diversions, from social media notifications to constant reading through news feeds, making it impossible to ignore. Individuals may become increasingly dependant on their cellphones to cope with stress, boredom, or loneliness, resulting in a difficult-to-break cycle of reliance.

The Rise in Smartphone Addiction

Smartphone addiction has become more prevalent in recent years, owing to technological advancements and broad availability of mobile devices. As cellphones become more intertwined into every part of contemporary life, it's no wonder that many people are unable to resist the attraction of continual communication.

One of the primary causes of smartphone addiction is the proliferation of social media platforms and their seductive design elements. Features like endless scrolling, push notifications, and likes and comments all contribute to a dopamine-driven feedback loop that keeps users coming back for more. When combined with the mobility and accessibility of smartphones, these capabilities allow people to spend hours every day hooked to their displays, frequently at the expense of other activities and duties.

Impact of Smartphone Addiction

While cellphones provide unrivaled convenience and connectedness, excessive usage can have a negative impact on our mental and emotional health. According to research, smartphone addiction is linked to a variety of undesirable outcomes, including:

1. Impaired Cognitive Function: Excessive smartphone use has been related to shorter attention spans, memory issues, and difficulties concentrating. Constantly moving between tasks and stimuli can strain the brain's cognitive resources, making it difficult to concentrate and remember information.

2. Negative Effects on Mental Health Smartphone addiction is frequently associated with emotions of worry, despair, and loneliness. Constantly comparing oneself to others on social media can worsen these thoughts and lead to feelings of inadequacy or FOMO (fear of missing out). Furthermore, the pressure to maintain a crafted online identity can cause feelings of inauthenticity and alienation from one's genuine self.

3. Disrupted sleep patterns: Smartphones produce blue light, which can disrupt the body's natural sleep-wake cycle, resulting in trouble falling asleep and poor sleep quality. Screen exposure before bedtime can reduce the

synthesis of melatonin, the hormone responsible for sleep regulation, making it more difficult to unwind and relax.

4. Strained Relationships Excessive smartphone use may result in the neglect of personal connections, as people prioritize their gadgets above spending meaningful time with loved ones. Constantly monitoring messages and social media feeds during meals or discussions can make loved ones feel overlooked or devalued, causing anger and conflict.

Identifying the Signs of Smartphone Addiction

Identifying smartphone addiction can be difficult since it frequently appears discreetly and gradually. However, there are some typical indications and symptoms to look for, including:

1. Excessive Screen Time: Spending a large chunk of the day on your smartphone, frequently at the expense of other things like work, school, or hobbies.

2. Preoccupation with the Device: Experiencing anxiety or restlessness while removed from your smartphone and continuously checking for notifications or updates. You may find yourself grabbing for your phone

compulsively, even when it is inappropriate or unnecessary.

3. Neglecting tasks: Ignoring key tasks like job, school, or housework in favor of utilizing your phone. You may struggle to concentrate on work or fulfill deadlines owing to continual interruptions from your device.

4. Interference with Relationships: Having disagreements with friends or family members as a result of excessive smartphone use, or feeling remote or alienated from loved ones. You may find yourself preferring your smartphone above spending meaningful time with loved ones, resulting in feelings of isolation and loneliness.

5. Negative Impact on Mental Health: Smartphone use may cause feelings of anxiety, despair, or poor self-esteem. You may find yourself comparing your life to others' on social media, leaving you feeling inadequate or uncomfortable. Furthermore, continual exposure to unpleasant news and information online can increase emotions of stress and overload.

Chapter 2:
The Science Behind Smartphone Addiction

Smartphones have grown omnipresent in modern life, acting as constant companions and key modes of communication, information access, and entertainment. While cellphones have obvious advantages, their excessive usage has generated worries about addiction and the possible damage on mental health and well-being. Understanding the science underlying smartphone addiction is critical for appreciating its complexities and developing effective preventative and response plans.

Neurological effects

The physiological impacts of smartphone addiction are linked to the brain's reward system, namely the release of dopamine, a neurotransmitter associated with pleasure and reward. When we participate in pleasurable or rewarding activities, such as utilizing our cellphones, dopamine is produced, causing emotions of happiness and reinforcement. This dopamine release reinforces the brain connections linked with the activity, making it more likely to occur again in the future.

Smartphones are intended to be extremely engaging, with features like alerts, social media updates, and interactive applications that cause dopamine release and keep users returning for more. The ongoing availability of fresh information and stimuli generates a condition of "intermittent reinforcement," in which users are rewarded in unpredictable ways, leading to increased expectation and addiction.

Furthermore, studies have found that excessive smartphone usage might cause anatomical and functional abnormalities in the brain. For example, neuroimaging studies have discovered changes in gray matter volume in parts of the brain involved in cognitive control and decision-making, such as the prefrontal cortex. These alterations may impair executive skills including impulse control and self-regulation, which can lead to addictive behaviors.

Furthermore, the blue light emitted by smartphone screens might interfere with the generation of melatonin, a hormone that governs sleep and waking cycles. Exposure to blue light, especially before bedtime, can reduce melatonin levels and disrupt sleep, thereby worsening addictive behavior.

Psychological Mechanisms

Psychological variables play an important part in smartphone addiction, impacting our motives, feelings, and behaviors. One such component is the idea of hedonic adaptation, which refers to people's proclivity to quickly adapt to enjoyable experiences and need higher amounts of stimulation to get the same degree of enjoyment. This behavior may lead to increased smartphone use as consumers seek more engaging material to satisfy their needs.

Furthermore, cellphones address a variety of psychological demands, including the desire for social connection, validation, and amusement. Social media platforms, in particular, offer a forum for social engagement and self-expression, with features such as likes, comments, and shares functioning as forms of social validation. The steady flood of messages and updates fosters a sense of connection and belonging, which reinforces addictive behaviors.

Furthermore, cellphones provide an escape from boredom, tension, or loneliness, often known as escapism. By immersing oneself in digital diversions, we might momentarily relieve bad feelings while avoiding tackling fundamental difficulties. However, this escape may become addictive, resulting in excessive smartphone usage and disengagement from real-world activities and relationships.

Behavioral Patterns

Smartphone addiction is characterized with excessive screen time, obsessive checking, and withdrawal symptoms when separated from the device. Excessive screen time is defined as spending a large amount of the day on a smartphone, frequently at the expense of other activities and duties. This conduct can interfere with job, education, and social interactions, resulting in severe repercussions in many aspects of life.

Another sign of smartphone addiction is compulsive checking, which is defined by a persistent urge to check for alerts, update social media feeds, or react to messages. This conduct is motivated by the desire for rewards and the fear of losing out on essential information or updates. Over time, constant monitoring can become engrained as a habit, making it tough to overcome smartphone addiction.

Individuals who are removed from their cellphones frequently experience withdrawal symptoms such as anxiety, irritation, or restlessness. These symptoms result from the interruption of regular behaviors and the removal of dopamine reinforcement, which causes discomfort and desires for the device. Withdrawal symptoms can exacerbate addictive behaviors as people try to lessen their agony by returning to their devices.

To summarize, the science underpinning smartphone addiction is a complex combination of neurological, psychological, and behavioral components. Understanding these fundamental principles allows us to create more effective therapies and methods for combating smartphone addiction and encouraging better technology usage. From setting screen time limitations to addressing underlying psychological needs, managing smartphone addiction necessitates a diversified strategy that takes into account the various elements that contribute to this rising issue.

Chapter 3:
Assessing Your Smartphone Habits

In our digital age, cellphones have become indispensable instruments for communication, information access, and entertainment. However, the widespread use of cellphones has generated worries about the risk of addiction, as well as the influence on mental health and wellbeing. Assessing your smartphone habits is an important first step toward better understanding your relationship with technology and identifying opportunities for development. In this part, we'll look at different methods for analyzing your smartphone habits, such as self-reflection activities, identifying problematic behaviors, and spotting trends and triggers.

Self-Reflection Exercises

Self-reflection activities are useful for obtaining insight into your smartphone habits and understanding the significance of technology in your life. Reflecting on your smartphone-related thoughts, feelings, and behaviors can help you uncover trends, triggers, and underlying reasons that may be contributing to problematic usage.

One self-reflection practice is to keep a smartphone journal, in which you record facts about your smartphone usage throughout the day. Take note of when you reach for your phone, what you do, and how you feel before and after using it. Pay attention to any patterns or trends that arise, such as times of day when you are more likely to use your smartphone or activities that result in excessive consumption.

Another useful self-reflection practice is the "Five Whys" approach, in which you continually ask yourself "why" to understand the underlying causes of your smartphone behaviors. For example, if you are continually checking social media, consider why you feel the need to do so. Perhaps you want to feel validated or connected to others, or you use social media to escape boredom or stress. By delving deeper into your reasons, you may better understand your smartphone behaviors and find opportunities for improvement.

Identifying problematic behaviors

Identifying problematic behaviors is an important step in evaluating your smartphone habits and identifying areas for improvement. Excessive screen time, compulsive checking, and failure to prioritize real-world responsibilities and relationships are examples of problematic behaviors. By identifying these behaviors, you can start addressing them and taking proactive steps toward healthier smartphone use.

One method for identifying problematic behaviors is to conduct a smartphone audit, which involves reviewing your usage patterns and assessing the impact of smartphone use on various aspects of your life. Take note of how much time you spend on your smartphone each day, as well as which apps and activities take up the most time. Be aware of any negative implications of smartphone use, such as lower productivity, interrupted sleep habits, or strained relationships with friends and family.

Another approach is to use smartphone tracking apps or built-in features to automatically track your usage patterns. These applications can give useful information about your smartphone habits, such as total screen time, app use statistics, and alerts received. Reviewing this data on a regular basis can help you detect trends and patterns in your smartphone usage and make educated decisions about where to direct your efforts for development.

Recognizing Patterns and Triggers

Understanding the underlying causes of problematic smartphone habits requires the recognition of patterns and triggers. Patterns may include times of day when you are more likely to use your smartphone, such as during meals or before bedtime, as well as activities that cause excessive use, such as boredom or stress. Recognizing these patterns and triggers allows you to develop more effective management strategies and reduce the likelihood of problematic smartphone use.

One approach to recognizing patterns and triggers is to create a behavior chain analysis, where you identify the antecedents (triggers), behaviors (smartphone use), and consequences (rewards) associated with your smartphone habits. For example, if you find yourself reaching for your phone whenever you feel bored, the boredom serves as the trigger, smartphone use is the behavior, and the distraction and entertainment provided by your device serve as the reward. By sketching out these chains, you may get insight into the variables that influence your smartphone behaviors and devise tactics to break them.

Another method is to practice mindfulness and self-awareness, which involves focusing on the present moment and observing your thoughts, feelings, and behaviors without judgment. Mindfulness exercises, such as mindful breathing or body scanning, can help you become more aware to your internal feelings and detect the impulses and cravings that lead to smartphone usage. By being aware of your patterns and the sensations connected with them, you may have more control over your smartphone usage and make more deliberate decisions about when and how to interact with it.

To summarize, examining your smartphone behaviors is an important first step toward understanding your relationship with technology and identifying opportunities for development. By engaging in self-reflection activities, identifying problematic behaviors, and detecting trends and triggers, you may gain insight into the reasons that drive your smartphone habits and create techniques for controlling them more successfully. By taking proactive efforts to create healthy smartphone habits, you may increase your well-being and reclaim control over your digital life.

Chapter 4:
The Consequences of Smartphone Addiction

As smartphones have grown more intertwined into our daily lives, the issue of smartphone addiction has arisen as a major worry. Excessive smartphone usage may have serious effects for many parts of our lives, including our relationships, productivity, and general health. In this part, we will go over the repercussions of smartphone addiction in depth, concentrating on the effects on relationships and social life, productivity and attention, and sleep and well-being.

Relationships and Social Life

One of the most serious repercussions of smartphone addiction is the strain on relationships and social interactions. Excessive smartphone usage can reduce face-to-face connection and involvement with others, as people become more absorbed with their gadgets and less aware of others around them.

For example, frequently checking notifications, reading through social media feeds, or replying to messages at social events can obstruct meaningful connection and degrade the quality of interpersonal interactions. Friends and family members may feel overlooked or devalued, which can lead to emotions of bitterness and isolation.

Moreover, smartphone addiction might prevent the formation of strong social ties and personal partnerships. Individuals who emphasize their cellphones above making real interactions with others may experience loneliness and isolation. A lack of social support can have a negative impact on mental health and well-being, aggravating symptoms of anxiety, sadness, and poor self-esteem.

Furthermore, the continual comparison and rivalry promoted by social media platforms can exacerbate emotions of jealously, insecurity, and inadequacy, straining relationships and causing interpersonal conflict. The curated photographs and highlight reels that appear on social media can set unreasonable standards and expectations, prompting people to doubt their own worth and value in comparison to others.

Smartphone addiction may have a significant impact on relationships and social life, reducing the quality of interpersonal contacts, impeding the formation of strong social ties, and leading to feelings of loneliness and isolation.

Productivity and focus

Another key implication of smartphone addiction is its influence on productivity and concentration. Excessive smartphone use can interfere with focus, impede cognitive function, and reduce productivity, making it harder to complete activities effectively and efficiently.

For example, continuously moving between tasks and distractions on a smartphone might fragment attention and impair capacity to focus on crucial tasks. According to studies, multitasking, which includes reading email, browsing the internet, and reacting to alerts at the same time, can diminish productivity by up to 40% while increasing the risk of errors and blunders.

The addictive nature of cellphones can result in obsessive monitoring and continuous interruptions throughout the day, reducing productivity and attention. The dopamine-driven reward system connected with smartphone use encourages the behavior, making it difficult to resist the want to check for updates and messages.

Also, excessive smartphone use can lead to procrastination and time-wasting habits, as people get preoccupied with mindless scrolling and digital diversions rather than participating in productive activities. Individuals may experience emotions of guilt, frustration, and overwhelm as they strive to meet deadlines and fulfill their goals.

To summarize, smartphone addiction can reduce productivity and attention, making it harder to complete activities effectively and efficiently. Individuals who are continually seeking diversions and disruptions may impair their capacity to concentrate and achieve their goals, resulting in negative effects in a variety of areas of life.

Sleep and Wellbeing

A third effect of smartphone addiction is that it interferes with sleep and overall well-being. Smartphone displays produce blue light, which can disturb the body's natural sleep-wake cycle and interfere with the generation of melatonin, the sleep-regulating hormone. Exposure to blue light before bedtime can reduce melatonin levels and delay the beginning of sleep, resulting in trouble falling asleep and poor sleep quality.

Also, the addictive nature of cellphones can cause nighttime procrastination as people become interested in their devices and lose sight of time. According to studies, using a smartphone before bedtime leads to shorter sleep duration, worse sleep efficiency, and more sleep disruptions.

Moreover, the continual stimulation and cognitive engagement given by smartphones might make it difficult for people to wind down and relax before going to bed. Instead of indulging in relaxing activities like reading or meditation, people may turn to their cellphones for amusement and distraction, worsening sleep issues.

In addition to its effect on sleep, smartphone addiction can have far-reaching consequences for general well-being. Excessive smartphone usage has been related to higher levels of stress, anxiety, and depression, as people struggle to detach from their gadgets and find balance in their lives. The continual pressure to be connected and available can lead to feelings of overload and burnout, which can have a severe impact on mental and emotional well-being.

Smartphone addiction can alter sleep patterns, affect general well-being, and increase feelings of stress and worry. Smartphone addiction, which disrupts the body's normal sleep-wake cycle and exacerbates feelings of stress, can have serious ramifications for mental health and quality of life.

Chapter 5:

Breaking the Cycle: Practical Strategies

In today's digital era, the widespread usage of cellphones has sparked increased worry about addiction and its effects on mental health and wellness. To break away from the smartphone addiction loop, we must take proactive efforts and use realistic tactics to recover control of our digital behaviors and create a better connection with technology. In this part, we will look at four main tactics for ending the cycle of smartphone addiction: setting boundaries and limitations, digital detox approaches, mindfulness and meditation practices, and developing offline interests and activities.

Establishing Boundaries and Limits

Setting boundaries and limits is an important first step toward stopping the cycle of smartphone addiction. Individuals may recover control of their digital habits and limit the danger of excessive usage by setting clear parameters for smartphone use and adhering to them regularly.

Setting specified time limitations for smartphone use throughout the day is an excellent method. Individuals may designate specific times of the day as "phone-free" time, such as during meals, family events, or before bedtime. Individuals can make space for meaningful relationships and emphasize offline activities by setting aside specific times when cellphones are not permitted.

Furthermore, establishing limits around certain applications or activities might help people lessen their dependency on cellphones and avoid distractions. Individuals, for example, may opt to disable alerts for non-essential applications, limit their social media usage to a particular amount of minutes per day, or utilize productivity tools to block distracting websites when working or studying.

Additionally, creating limitations for smartphone usage in certain contexts, such as the bedroom or the office, might help people develop a feeling of separation between their digital and physical lives. Individuals may create opportunities for relaxation, attention, and connection by designating specific areas as "phone-free zones," eliminating the continual presence of digital distractions.

Digital Detox Techniques

Digital detox approaches entail taking deliberate pauses from smartphones and other digital gadgets to recharge, reconnect with the present moment, and cultivate increased mindfulness and awareness. These approaches can help people stop the cycle of smartphone addiction and reclaim a sense of balance and perspective in their life.

One popular digital detox strategy is the "unplugged weekend," in which people pledge to going without cellphones or other digital gadgets for the whole weekend. Individuals can use this time to participate in offline activities such as spending time in nature, reading physical books, or pursuing creative hobbies. Disconnecting from technology allows people to replenish their mental and emotional batteries while also gaining a newfound appreciation for their surroundings.

Another successful digital detox strategy is the "technology fast," in which people refrain from using cellphones and other digital gadgets for a specific amount of time, such as a day, week, or month. This enables people to break free from the continual stimulation and distraction of technology, reclaiming their time and attention for more meaningful activities.

Furthermore, implementing frequent digital detox rituals into daily or weekly routines might help people develop healthy behaviors and lower their risk of smartphone addiction. Individuals may select mindfulness methods such as meditation, yoga, or deep breathing exercises to enhance relaxation and mental clarity. Individuals who take the time to withdraw from technology and reconnect with themselves can stop the cycle of smartphone addiction and promote improved well-being.

Mindfulness and meditation practices

Mindfulness and meditation activities are effective tools for stopping the cycle of smartphone addiction while also building better awareness and presence in our lives. Individuals may increase their self-awareness and make more deliberate decisions regarding their smartphone usage by learning to monitor their thoughts, feelings, and behaviors without judgment.

One basic mindfulness practice is to take a few moments each day to halt, breathe, and check in with ourselves. This may be as easy as taking a few deep breaths, paying attention to any bodily sensations, and analyzing the ideas and emotions that come. By raising awareness of our interior sensations, we may begin to get better clarity and insight into how smartphone addiction may be affecting our lives.

Another successful mindfulness technique is mindful eating, which involves savoring and appreciating each piece of food without distraction. Turning off cellphones and other digital gadgets during meals allows people to make more room for mindful eating and develop a stronger connection to the sensory experience of eating.

Furthermore, adopting formal meditation techniques into everyday routines might assist individuals improve their mental clarity, emotional resilience, and self-regulation. Mindfulness meditation, loving-kindness meditation, and body scan meditation can help people become more aware of their thoughts, feelings, and actions, as well as minimize the compulsive impulse to check their cellphones all the time.

Promoting Offline Hobbies and Activities

Cultivating offline interests and activities is another important method for breaking the cycle of smartphone addiction and increasing fulfillment and pleasure in our life. Individuals may lessen their dependency on cellphones by choosing activities that provide joy, purpose, and fulfillment outside of the digital domain, allowing them to interact and engage with the world around them.

One method is to pursue hobbies and interests that foster creativity, self-expression, and personal development. This might include activities like painting, writing, gardening, or playing musical instruments, which allow people to disengage from technology and participate in things that offer them joy and satisfaction.

Likewise, spending time in nature may be a potent cure to smartphone addiction since it provides opportunities for relaxation.

Reflection and renewal. Hiking, camping, or simply spending time outside can help people reconnect with nature and build a sense of awe and wonder that extends beyond the limitations of their cellphones.

Besides, making meaningful relationships with others through in-person encounters and community activities might help people overcome the isolation and separation caused by smartphone addiction. Whether it's joining a sports team, working for a local charity, or attending social events and gatherings, offline activities may help people form deeper social links and feel a feeling of belonging and connection in their life.

Worthy of note, ending the cycle of smartphone addiction necessitates proactive steps and realistic tactics for regaining control of our digital behaviors and cultivating a healthy connection with technology. Individuals can overcome smartphone addiction by setting boundaries and restrictions, using digital detox approaches, embracing mindfulness and meditation practices, and creating offline interests and activities.

Chapter 6:
Navigating Social Media and Digital Culture

How to Navigate Social Media and Digital Culture

In today's linked world, social media and digital culture have a tremendous impact on how we interact and consume information, as well as how we develop and sustain connections. While social media has various advantages, such as promoting social relationships and providing access to a multitude of information, it also introduces new obstacles and complications. Navigating social media and digital culture demands careful analysis and creative techniques to ensure that our online interactions benefit our general well-being. In this part, we'll look at three important areas of navigating social media and digital culture: social media management, FOMO (Fear of Missing Out), and developing healthy online connections.

Manage Social Media Use

Managing social media usage is critical for striking a good balance between our online and offline lives. With a continual stream of updates, notifications, and information competing for our attention, it's easy to become engrossed in the endless scroll of social media platforms and lose sight of our goals and ideals. Individuals may limit the negative consequences of excessive social media use by applying effective management tactics, as well as cultivating a more purposeful and thoughtful attitude to online interactions.

Establishing clear boundaries and restrictions on when and how we participate with social media platforms is an excellent method for regulating our social media use. This might include setting daily time limitations for social media use, designating particular times of the day as "screen-free" hours, or taking frequent breaks from social media entirely. We may lessen the likelihood of obsessive social media use and regain control of our digital lives by setting boundaries.

Likewise, organizing our social media feeds to represent our beliefs and interests might contribute to a more enjoyable and meaningful online experience. This might include unfollowing accounts that encourage negativity or comparison, muting phrases or themes that elicit negative feelings, or actively searching out content that inspires, informs, or raises us. By surrounding ourselves with information that reflects our beliefs and interests, we may create a more supportive and rewarding online community.

Furthermore, exercising digital mindfulness and self-awareness can help people become more aware of their social media habits and how they affect their mental and emotional health. This may entail occasionally reflecting on our reasons for using social media, observing how various sorts of material make us feel, and being careful of how much time and energy we devote to our online relationships. By being more aware of our social media usage habits, we may make better educated decisions regarding when and how we interact with these sites.

Managing FOMO (Fear of Missing Out)

Handling FOMO (Fear of Missing Out) is an important part of navigating social media and digital culture. FOMO is the fear or nervousness that people feel when they are excluded from social activities, experiences, or chances that others are taking part in. Social media services intensify FOMO by giving a steady stream of updates and highlights from other people's life, causing people to compare themselves negatively and feel inadequate or insecure.

One helpful method for dealing with FOMO is to be grateful and appreciative of what we have rather than focused on what we are missing out on. Individuals who cultivate a grateful mentality can shift their attention from comparison and lack to plenty and joy. This may include keeping a thankfulness diary in which people frequently write down things they're grateful for, or just spending a moment each day to reflect on the gifts and advantages in their lives.

In addition, shifting our viewpoint on social media might help reduce FOMO and encourage a more balanced and realistic picture of others' lives. Recognizing that social media delivers a filtered and edited version of reality rather than an authentic portrayal of others' lives might help people keep their perspective and avoid slipping into the comparison trap. Individuals may create greater compassion and self-compassion by recognizing that everyone has struggles and disappointments, not just those we see on social media.

Furthermore, exercising self-care and self-compassion is critical for coping with FOMO and maintaining emotional stability. This may include putting limits on our social media usage to avoid comparison and overload, prioritizing activities and relationships that offer us joy and fulfillment, and engaging in stress-reduction methods like meditation, mindfulness, or physical exercise. We may create better confidence and self-assurance by caring for ourselves and prioritizing our own wants and ideals, reducing the influence of FOMO on our life.

Creating Healthy Online Relationships

Building healthy online interactions is another critical component of managing social media and digital culture. While social media platforms provide new potential for connection and community development, they also provide unique obstacles and concerns, such as cyberbullying, online harassment, and the spread of disinformation. Individuals may develop healthy and good online connections, resulting in a friendly and inclusive online community that values mutual respect, empathy, and understanding.

One critical component of developing successful online connections is prioritizing honesty and openness in our interactions. This entails communicating in an honest and real manner, expressing our ideas, feelings, and experiences honestly and truthfully, and treating people with respect and empathy. Individuals may establish deeper and more meaningful relationships with others while also creating a feeling of belonging and community online by cultivating an environment of trust and vulnerability.

Additionally, developing digital empathy and compassion is critical for maintaining good online interactions and cultivating a culture of kindness and respect. This includes thinking about the influence of our words and actions on others, carefully listening to their viewpoints and experiences, and providing support and encouragement as required. Individuals may foster a friendly and inclusive online community that celebrates diversity and encourages mutual understanding by demonstrating empathy and compassion in their online interactions.

Setting boundaries and exercising digital self-care are critical for sustaining good online interactions and safeguarding our mental and emotional wellbeing. This may entail creating guidelines for acceptable behavior and communication, such as refraining from engaging in online arguments or conflicts, blocking or unfriending people who engage in harmful or abusive behavior, and prioritizing our own needs and boundaries in our online interactions. Setting boundaries and caring for ourselves can help us create a safer and more helpful online environment for ourselves and others.

To abridge, managing social media and digital culture demands careful analysis and smart measures to ensure that our online interactions contribute favorably to our overall well-being. Individuals may establish a more purposeful and conscious attitude to their digital lives by regulating their social media use, dealing with FOMO, and developing good online interactions, resulting in a supportive and inclusive online community that encourages mutual respect, empathy, and understanding.

Chapter 7:

Tools and Resources for Recovery

Overcoming smartphone addiction necessitates a multifaceted strategy that combines self-help techniques and external support networks. Fortunately, there are several tools and services available to help folks on their recovery path. In this part, we will look at three major types of recovery tools and resources: applications and tools for restricting usage, support groups and communities, and professional treatment and therapy.

Apps and Tools to Limit Usage

In recent years, there has been an increase in the creation of applications and technologies that assist people regulate their smartphone usage and break free from compulsive habits. These applications include a variety of features and capabilities intended at encouraging attentive and purposeful smartphone use while lowering the danger of excessive usage.

Time-tracking and monitoring applications are a popular type of tool that allows users to measure their screen time and establish use limitations. Moment, Screen Time, and QualityTime apps let users understand their smartphone behaviors, such as total screen time, app usage data, and notifications. Users may establish daily use targets, receive reminders when they exceed them, and monitor their progress over time.

Distraction-blocking applications are another type of tool that helps users stay focused on their work and objectives by minimizing distractions. Apps like Freedom, Forest, and Cold Turkey Blocker enable users to restrict access to distracting websites and apps for certain periods of time, allowing them to focus on work, school, or other tasks without interruption. Some applications even utilize gamification, awarding users with virtual trees or cash for being focused and avoiding distractions.

Also, there are apps particularly developed to enhance digital awareness and lessen the obsessive need to check cellphones. Apps like Headspace, Calm, and Insight Timer provide guided meditation sessions, relaxation exercises, and mindfulness practices to help users develop better awareness and presence in their life. By adding mindfulness into their everyday routines, people may create better behaviors and break the cycle of smartphone addiction.

Support Groups and Communities

Support groups and communities can help people recover by offering encouragement, accountability, and understanding from those who have had similar struggles. encouragement groups, whether in person or online, provide a safe and friendly environment for people to express their challenges, seek direction and encouragement, and celebrate their progress toward recovery.

12-step programs, such as Smartphone Addiction Anonymous (SAA) or Internet and Technology Addicts Anonymous (ITAA), are a common type of support group. These programs take a systematic approach based on Alcoholics Anonymous concepts, such as acknowledging powerlessness over addiction, submitting to a higher power, and taking moral responsibility for one's behavior. Meetings usually include sharing personal experiences, discussing recovery tactics, and providing support and encouragement to other members.

Likewise, internet forums and groups provide an excellent platform for people to communicate with one another, exchange resources and methods, and seek advice and help on their recovery path. Websites like Reddit, PsychCentral, and SMART Recovery provide online forums and discussion groups for issues including smartphone addiction, digital detox, and technology usage. These forums enable people to anonymously discuss their stories, ask questions, and receive support and encouragement from others who understand their difficulties.

Furthermore, social media platforms such as Facebook and Twitter may function as virtual support networks, allowing people to connect with others who share their interests, join recovery and wellness groups, and engage in online events. Individuals might feel less alone in their recovery path by connecting with others who share similar objectives and problems, as well as receive inspiration and encouragement from other people's successes.

Professional Support and Counseling

Individuals living with severe or chronic smartphone addiction may require professional assistance and therapy in order to address underlying issues and create appropriate coping mechanisms. Therapists, counselors, and psychologists can give specialized assistance and guidance based on an individual's specific needs and circumstances.

Cognitive-behavioral therapy (CBT) is one of the most popular techniques to treating smartphone addiction because it helps people identify and address maladaptive ideas and behaviors linked with addiction. CBT teaches people coping skills and techniques for managing urges, regulating emotions, and breaking the cycle of addictive behaviors. Therapists may also use mindfulness-based treatments, such as mindfulness meditation and acceptance and commitment therapy (ACT), to assist patients develop more self-awareness and compassion.

Also, addiction treatment institutes and rehab facilities provide specialized programs and assistance for people dealing with smartphone addiction and other technology-related problems. These programs often include individual treatment, group counseling, education sessions, and experiential activities aimed at promoting recovery and wellbeing. Inpatient and outpatient treatment options are available, depending on the severity of the addiction and the individual's treatment need.

Furthermore, family therapy and support can be good for those suffering from smartphone addiction since it addresses family dynamics and communication patterns that may lead to or worsen addictive behaviors. Family therapy sessions provide a safe and supportive environment for family members to voice their concerns, practice good communication skills, and collaborate to assist the individual in their recovery path.

To summarize, resolving smartphone addiction necessitates a comprehensive and integrated strategy that addresses both the individual's internal difficulties and external support networks. Individuals may learn the skills and tactics necessary to break free from addictive habits and establish a better connection with technology by utilizing tools and resources such as applications and tools for restricting usage, support groups and communities, and professional aid and therapy. Recovery is attainable, whether via self-help tactics or external support networks, and people may regain control of their digital lives while also rediscovering a sense of balance and well-being.

[57]

Chapter 8:

Creating a Sustainable Digital Lifestyle

In today's fast-paced digital environment, developing a sustainable digital lifestyle is critical for achieving balance, well-being, and productivity. A sustainable digital lifestyle entails developing healthy habits, balancing technology usage, and setting long-term objectives to ensure that our interaction with technology improves rather than degrades our quality of life. In this part, we will look at the fundamental factors of developing a sustainable digital lifestyle and offer practical advice and tactics for doing so.

Developing Healthy Habits

Establishing healthy habits is the cornerstone of a long-term digital lifestyle. By introducing thoughtful and purposeful activities into our everyday routines, we may create better awareness and balance in our interactions with technology. Here are some recommendations for developing healthy habits:

1. Attentive Tech Use: When using technology, be attentive of how it makes you feel and if it is consistent with your values and priorities.

2. Screen Time Boundaries: Limit your screen time and set aside certain times to withdraw from digital gadgets and focus on other things.

3. Tech-Free Zones: Establish tech-free zones in your house or workplace where cellphones and other gadgets are not permitted, such as the bedroom or dining room.

4. Digital Detoxes: Plan frequent digital detoxes in which you disconnect from technology for a specific amount of time to rejuvenate and reconnect with the offline world.

5. Tech-Free Activities: To balance your screen time, engage in non-technological activities like as reading a book, going for a walk, or spending time with loved ones.

By adding these healthy behaviors into your daily routine, you may mitigate the negative impacts of excessive technology usage while also creating a more sustainable and balanced digital lifestyle.

Balanced Technology Use

Balancing technology use is critical for leading a sustainable digital lifestyle. While technology provides several benefits and conveniences, it is critical to consider the influence it has on our mental, emotional, and physical health. Here are some recommendations for balancing your technology use.

1. Prioritize Offline Interactions: Set aside time for in-person interactions with friends and family members, as well as offline activities and hobbies that offer you joy and fulfillment.

2. Limit Multitasking: Multitasking with technology might reduce productivity and cognitive function. Instead, give each work your complete attention.

3. Practice Digital Sabbaticals: Take frequent vacations from technology, such as weekends or nights, to recharge and refocus. Use this time to do offline activities and reconnect with yourself and others.

4. Establish Clear Work-Life Boundaries: Set certain times when you will not read work emails or communications. Instead than letting technology dominate all of your time and attention, use it to increase your productivity and efficiency.

5. Use Technology Mindfully: Be deliberate about how you use technology, selecting applications and gadgets that reflect your beliefs and aspirations. Avoid idle scrolling and instead utilize technology to enrich your life, not as a continual distraction.

By balancing your technology use and emphasizing offline activities, you may live a more sustainable and meaningful digital lifestyle that promotes well-being and happiness.

Establishing Long-term Goals

Setting long-term objectives is critical for developing a sustainable digital lifestyle that reflects your beliefs and aspirations. By defining success for yourself and creating specific goals for your digital habits and behaviors, you can stay focused and motivated to achieve your goals. Here are some suggestions for setting long-term goals:

1. Reflect on Your Values: Take some time to focus on your values, priorities, and what is most important to you in life. Consider how technology relates to your values and identify areas where you want to make adjustments or enhancements.

2. Identify Areas for Improvement: Evaluate your existing technological routines and behaviors to determine where you want to make adjustments or improvements. This might involve limiting screen time, practising mindfulness, or developing digital literacy.

3. Set SMART objectives: Use the SMART criteria (Specific, Measurable, Achievable, Relevant, and Time-bound) to establish clear and practical objectives for your digital lifestyle. Break down major goals into smaller, more achievable tasks, and monitor your progress over time.

4. Make a Plan: Create a strategy for accomplishing your long-term objectives, including specific activities you will take, resources you will require, and potential roadblocks. Be open to change your plan in response to comments and fresh information.

5. Seek Support and Accountability: Share your objectives with friends, family, or a support group, and solicit their help and encouragement to achieve them. Consider collaborating with an accountability buddy to help you stay on track and motivated.

Setting long-term objectives for your digital lifestyle and taking proactive efforts to attain them can help you develop a sustainable and rewarding relationship with technology that improves your general well-being and quality of life.

To recap, maintaining a sustainable digital lifestyle takes deliberate work and dedication to developing healthy habits, balancing technology usage, and defining long-term objectives. By adding mindful practices into your daily routines, prioritizing offline experiences, and defining specific goals for your digital habits, you may build a more balanced and gratifying relationship with technology that promotes well-being and happiness. Remember that developing a healthy digital lifestyle is a continuous process, and it is OK to change your approach as necessary along the way. By remaining conscious and purposeful in your behaviors, you may establish a long-term digital lifestyle that supports your beliefs and objectives.

Conclusion

Examining the many components of smartphone addiction and the tactics for breaking free from its grip reveals that the ubiquitous impact of technology in our lives necessitates careful thinking and decisive action. Smartphone addiction, with its neurological, psychological, and behavioral consequences, presents substantial hurdles to anyone seeking a balanced and fulfilled life in today's digital era.

However, these obstacles also chances for development, resilience, and recovering control over our digital habits. Individuals may traverse the complexity of smartphone addiction and construct a route to long-term digital well-being by developing self-awareness, taking active action, and making use of accessible services.

Recognizing the existence and influence of smartphones on our life is the first step toward breaking away from their addiction. Individuals can begin their recovery journey by understanding the indicators of addiction and its underlying causes. This path is not without challenges, as cellphones' addictive nature and the widespread impact of digital culture provide tremendous impediments to change.

Individuals, with drive and dedication, may apply realistic tactics for limiting smartphone usage, growing mindfulness, and developing healthy behaviors. There are several ways to retake control over our digital lives, including setting boundaries and restrictions on technology usage, participating in digital detoxes, and prioritizing offline activities.

Furthermore, community support, both online and offline, may be useful in terms of encouragement, direction, and solidarity during the healing process. Individuals can gain strength in community by sharing their stories, receiving guidance, and providing mutual support, recognizing that they are not alone in their challenges.

Also, professional assistance and therapy can provide further support and direction to people struggling with severe or chronic smartphone addiction. Therapeutic therapies, such as cognitive-behavioral therapy and addiction treatment programs, can provide people with the tools and resources they need to address underlying difficulties and establish healthy coping mechanisms.

In order to live a sustainable digital lifestyle, self-care, balance, and general well-being must be prioritized. Individuals may have a more purposeful and rewarding relationship with technology by making meaningful relationships with people, participating in offline activities, and creating long-term objectives for their digital habits.

Ultimately, breaking away from smartphone addiction is a continuous process of self-discovery and progress. It takes patience, effort, and a willingness to face obstacles and uncertainties along the route. However, with dedication and a commitment to live in accordance with our values and goals, we can break free from the grasp of smartphone addiction and develop a life that is balanced, meaningful, and enriched by technology rather than controlled by it.